CLASSICAL ARABIC WRITTEN

A1-C1

AUTHORED

JACOB ELI GOODSON

CALEB ELI GOODSON

EDITOR

CLASSICAL ARABIC WRITTEN

CONTENTS

0. General

1. The alphabet

2. Non-connectors

3. Short vowels

4. Long vowels

5. ʔálif maqṣúurah

6. Nunation

7. sukúun

8. šáddah

9. Non-connectors following another letter

10. Connected letters

11. síin

12. šíin

13. káaf

14. láam

15. míim

16. báaʔ

17. yáaʔ

18. núun

19. táaʔ

20. θáaʔ

21. háaʔ

22. táaʔ marbúuṭah

23. hámzah with ʔálif

24. fáaʔ

25. qáaf

26. jíim

27. ʜáaʔ

28. xáaʔ

29. máddah

30. ʕáyn

31. g̃áyn

32. ṭáaʔ

33. ð̣áaʔ

34. ṣáad

35. ḍáad

36. hámzah

37. A special way of indicating long aa

38. Pause forms

39. Grammatical considerations

40. Verb forms with a final ʔálif

41. The prefix for "the"

42. Variant forms of the prefix for "the"

43. hámzatu‿lwáṣl

CLASSICAL WRITTEN ARABIC

0. Arabic is customarily written and printed in a special alphabet of its own, called the Arabic alphabet, consisting of 28 LETTERS and a number of SIGNS. Some of the salient features of this alphabet are as follows:

1. Arabic is written and printed from right to left.
2. Normally only the consonants and the long vowels are indicated.
3. There are no capital letters.
4. The manner of writing is cursive and most of the letters are connected to preceding and following letters within the same word.
5. Most of the letters have three or more variant shapes, depending on whether they are connected to preceding and/or following letters or not.
6. Some letters are identical in basic form and are distinguished from one another by small dots.
7. The system of writing described here is the handwriting commonly used in the Syrian area. In other parts of the Arab world, and in Iran, the handwriting styles vary from slightly to considerably different. Printing types also vary, some being quite complex and ornate.

1. The alphabet

The following list shows the letters of the Arabic alphabet in the shape they have when they stand alone, that is, not connected to a preceding or following letter. This is the order of the alphabet adopted by most dictionaries. The signs will be discussed later.

Usual sound value	Arabic name	Arabic letter
ʔ, aa	ʔálif	ا
b	báaʔ	ب
t	táaʔ	ت <u>or</u> ت
θ	θáaʔ	ث <u>or</u> ث

Usual sound value	Arabic name	Arabic Letter
j	jíim	ج
ħ	ħáa?	ح
x	xáa?	خ
d	dáal	د
ð	ðáal	ذ
r	ráa?	ر
z	záay	ز
s	síin	ـسـ or س
š	šíin	ـشـ or ش
ṣ	ṣáad	ص
ḍ	ḍáad	ض
ṭ	ṭáa?	ط
ð̣	ð̣áa?	ظ
ʕ	ʕáyn	ع
ğ	ğáyn	غ
f	fáa?	ف
q	qáaf	ق or ق

Usual sound value	Arabic name	Arabic Letter
k	káaf	ك or ك
l	láam	ل
m	míim	م
n	núun	ن
h	háaʔ	ه or ه
w , uu	wáaw	و
y , ii	yáaʔ	ي or ي

The following shows the Arabic letters in their alphabetical order and written from right to left. Note the placing of the letters relative to the line of writing.

ا ب ت ث ج ح خ د ذ ر ز س ش ص ض

ط ظ ع غ ف ق ك ل م ن ه و ي

2. The following 6 letters are NON-CONNECTORS. They do not form a cursive linking to a following letter, though they do connect to a preceding letter other than another non-connector.

- ا ʔálif is characteristically a vertical stroke
- د dáal
- ذ ðáal is exactly like dáal, but with one dot above it
- ر ráaʔ
- ز záay is exactly like ráaʔ, but with one dot above it
- و wáaw

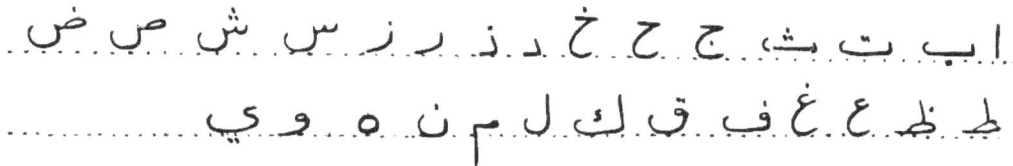

3. Short vowels

dárasa	دَرَسَ	dáraka	دَرَكَ
wárada	وَرَدَ	rázaqa	رَزَقَ
wázara	وَزَرَ	wádaʕa	وَدَعَ
wáraša	وَرَشَ	wázana	وَزَنَ

All the above words show the sign َ fátħah above each consonant letter. This sign indicates that each consonant is followed by the vowel a.

wúzina	وُزِنَ	wúriθa	وُرِثَ
wúzira	وُزِرَ	wúdiʕa	وُدِعَ
rúziqa	رُزِقَ	dúrika	دُرِكَ
wúrida	وُرِدَ	dúrisa	دُرِسَ

All the above words show the sign ُ dámmah above the first consonant letter. This sign indicates that the consonant is followed by the vowel u.

All these words also show the sign ِ kásrah below the second consonant letter. This sign indicates that the consonant is followed by the vowel i.

4. Long vowels

záala	زَالَ	ðáaqa	ذَاقَ
záara	زَارَ	ðáata	ذَاتَ
záada	زَادَ	ráaja	رَاجَ
dáana	دَانَ	ráaʕa	رَاعَ

záağa	زَاغَ	dáara	دَارَ
dáama	دَامَ	wáaʜa	وَاحَ
ráaʜa	رَاحَ	ðáaba	ذَابَ
ráaqa	رَاقَ	ráama	رَامَ

All the above words show a consonant with the sign َ fátʜah immediately followed by an ا ʔálif. This sequence indicates that the consonant is followed by the long vowel aa.

rúuʜu	رُوحُ	ðúu	ذُو
zúuru	زُورُ	dúumu	دُومُ
dúuru	دُورُ	dúuna	دُونَ
dúuju	دُوجُ	rúuʕu	رُوعُ

All the above words show a consonant with the sign ُ dámmah immediately followed by a و wáaw. This sequence indicates that the consonant is followed by the long vowel uu.

wáadii	وَادِي	ðíi	ذِي
dáarii	دَارِي	zúurii	زُورِي
		dúurii	دُورِي

All the above words show a consonant with the sign ِ kásrah immediately followed by a ي yáaʔ. This sequence indicates that the consonant is followed by the long vowel ii.

5. ʔálif maqṣúurah

wáraa	وَرَى	dáraa	دَرَى
dáwaa	دَوَى	wádaa	وَدَى
dáaraa	دَارَى	rádaa	رَدَى
		ráwaa	رَوَى

All the above words show a consonant with the sign َ fátḥah immediately followed by an undotted ى yáaʔ. This sequence indicates that the consonant is followed by the long vowel aa.

This way of indicating the long vowel aa occurs only at the end of a word. It is called ʔálif maqṣúurah. You will have to learn individually the words that are written with ʔálif maqṣúurah instead of with ا ʔálif (cf. Section 4) as there is no general rule to follow.

6. Nunation

rudúudun	رُدُودٌ	dáarun	دَارٌ
dúwalun	دُوَلٌ	wáaridun	وَارِدٌ
wurúudun	وُرُودٌ	wáraqun	وَرَقٌ
wáariθun	وَارِثٌ	zawáalun	زَوَالٌ
wadáaʕun	وَدَاعٌ	dawáamun	دَوَامٌ

All the above words show the sign ٌ ḍammatáan 'two ḍammahs' above the last consonant. This sign indicates the ending -un. This sign is also written as ٌ and ٌ .

rúuʜin	رُوحٍ	dáahin	دَاهٍ
wáafin	وَافٍ	ráaʕin	رَاعٍ
wáalin	وَالٍ	wáadin	وَادٍ
dámin	دَمٍ	dúwalin	دُوَلٍ
dáarin	دَارٍ	zawáajin	زَوَاجٍ

All the above words show the sign ٍ kasratáan 'two kasrahs' below the last consonant. This sign indicates the ending -in.

wáaridan	وَارِدًا	dáaran	دَارًا
zúuran	زُورًا	rudúudan	رُدُودًا
wurúudan	وُرُودًا	dúuran	دُورًا

All the above words show the sign ً fatʜatáan 'two fatʜahs' above the last consonant. This sign indicates the ending -an. The sign ً fatʜatáan usually occurs with an ا ʔálif, as in these examples. Note that here the letter ا ʔálif does not indicate the long vowel aa.

The n of these endings as well as this method of indicating it is called NUNATION; the Arabic term is tanwíin. Nunation occurs only at the end of a word.

rádan	رَدًى	wázan	وَزًى
ríwan	رِوًى	dáwan	دَوًى

The above words show the sign ً fatʜatáan over a consonant that is immediately followed by an undotted ى yáaʔ. You will have to learn the relatively few words that are written this way instead of with an ا ʔálif, as there is no general rule to follow.

7. **sukúun**

ráy	رَيْ	dárbun	دَرْبٌ
zúrtu	زُرْتُ	wáznun	وَزْنٌ
dársun	دَرْسٌ	záwjun	زَوْجٌ
zárʕun	زَرْعٌ	dáwrun	دَوْرٌ
wáy	وَيْ	wárdun	وَرْدٌ

All the above words show the sign ْ sukúun above the second consonant. This indicates that the consonant has no following vowel. This sign is also called jázmah.

8. **šáddah**

ráddada	رَدَّدَ	dábbun	دَبٌّ
dáallun	دَالٌّ	wáddun	وَدٌّ
záwwaja	زَوَّجَ	dálla	دَلَّ
zuwwáarun	زُوَّارٌ	ðábbun	ذَبٌّ
wázzaʕa	وَزَّعَ	rábbun	رَبٌّ

All the above words show the sign ّ šáddah over the second consonant. This sign indicates that the consonant is doubled. The process of doubling a consonant is called tašdíid and this term is also used to refer to the sign.

9. Non-connectors following another letter

The letter ل láam, when connected to a following letter only, has the form لـ . This letter will be discussed in detail in Section 14.

1. l connected to d

ládaa	لَدَى	ládaġa	لَدَغَ
wáladun	وَلَدٌ	wáladat	وَلَدَتْ

2. l connected to ð

láðaʕa	لَذَعَ	láðða	لَذَّ
láðaba	لَذَبَ	láðima	لَذِمَ

3. l connected to r

lirábbin	لِرَبٍّ	liráaʕin	لِراعٍ
lirúuḥin	لِرُوحٍ	lirízqin	لِرِزْقٍ

4. l connected to z

lázima	لَزِمَ	luzúumun	لُزُومٌ
lizáamun	لِزَامٌ	zálzala	زَلْزَلَ

5. l connected to w

láw	لَوْ	láwḥun	لَوْحٌ
láwwaθa	لَوَّثَ	láwnun	لَوْنٌ

6. l connected to ʔálif has a special form

záalaa	زَالَا	láa	لَا
dúwalan	دُوَلًا	láaḥa	لَاحَ
daláalun	دَلَالٌ	láazama	لَازَمَ

10. Connected letters

Most of the letters have three or more variant shapes, depending on their position in a sequence of letters, that is, whether they stand at the beginning, in the middle, or at the end of the sequence, or stand alone. Many letters, when standing at the end of a sequence or alone, have a variant with a flourishing final stroke. The variant with the flourish is often quite different from the other variants of the same letter.

In the following sections each letter will be taken up separately and the variant shapes will be given in the following order.

1. Connected to the following letter only.
2. Connected to the preceding and following letters.
3. Connected to the preceding letter only.
4. Standing alone.

11. The letter س síin is characteristically a series of three upward pointed strokes. In handwriting the three upward strokes are usually omitted and the letter is a horizontal straight line.

1. s- connected to the following letter only

sudúudun	سُدُودٌ	sárra	سَرَّ
síwaa	سِوَى	sáawaa	سَاوَى
sáara	سَارَ	rasúulun	رَسُولٌ

2. -s- connected to the preceding and following letters

lisiráajin	لِسِرَاجٍ	lisáanun	لِسَانٌ
lisúuqin	لِسُوقٍ	lásada	لَسَدَ
lisáddin	لِسَدٍّ	lásaa	لَسَا

3. -s connected to the preceding letter only

dállasa	دَلَّسَ	lássa	لَسَّ
		dássasa	دَسَّسَ

4. s standing alone

lawwáasun	لَوَّاسٌ	sáadisun	سَادِسٌ
durúusun	دُرُوسٌ	dársun	دَرْسٌ

Additional examples.

سَدَرَ	رَسَّامٌ	سُوَّاقٌ
سُرُورٌ	سَادَتْ	سَاذِجٌ
سَاغَ	سُدْسٌ	سَامٍ
دَرْسًا	رُسُومٍ	رَسْوٌ

12. The letter ش šíin has the same basic form as the letter س síin, but with the addition of three dots above it. In handwriting the dots are usually connected, forming a small tent-like mark.

1. š- connected to the following letter only

šáddat	شَدَّتْ	šáaraka	شَارَكَ
šárṭun	شَرْطٌ	šárafun	شَرَفٌ
šáwqun	شَوْقٌ	šárqin	شَرْقٍ

2. -š- connected to the preceding and following letters

lišáariʕin	لِشَارِعٍ	lišáwqin	لِشَوْقٍ
lášwan	لَشْوًا	lišárafin	لِشَرَفٍ

3. -š connected to the preceding letter only

		lášša	لَشَّ

4. š standing alone

wáraša	وَرَشَ	rášša	رَشَّ
rišáašun	رِشَاشٌ	láaša	لَاشَ

Additional examples.

شَرَعَ   شَرَّفَ   شَدَّدَ

رُشْدٌ   وَشَى   شَرَحَ

شُرُوطٌ   شَوَارِعُ   لِشَرْطٍ

13. The letter ك káaf is characteristically a vertical stroke with a slanting line connecting to the top from the right.

1. k- connected to the following letter only

káðaa	كَذَا	ðákara	ذَكَرَ
kárrama	كَرَّمَ	kiráamun	كِرَامٌ
wákadat	وَكَدَتْ	káwnun	كَوْنٌ

2. -k- connected to the preceding and following letters

sukúutin	سُكُوتٍ	šúkran	شُكْرًا
lákaša	لَكَشَ	sukúunun	سُكُونٌ
šákara	شَكَرَ	súkkarun	سُكَّرٌ

3. -k connected to the preceding letter only

síkakum	سِكَكُمْ	šákka	شَكَّ
wáškum	وَشْكُمْ	láka	لَكَ

4. k standing alone

dáraka	دَرَكَ	šukúukum	شُكُوكُمْ
šárraka	شَرَّكَ	ðáaka	ذَاكَ

5. káaf plus ʔálif has a special form

rukkáabun	رُكَّابٌ	káana	كَانَ
šákkan	شَكًّا	sukkáanun	سُكَّانٌ

Additional examples.

كَذَّبَ	ذَكَرَتْ	سَكَّرَتْ
كَافٍ	كَوَارِثُ	كَرْةٌ
كَوَّنَ	كَادَ	وَكْرٌ

14. The letter ل láam is characteristically a vertical stroke. It differs from ا ʔálif chiefly by connecting to a following letter.

1. l- connected to the following letter only

láδδa	لَذَّ	láw	لَوْ
láwnin	لَوْنٍ	lázima	لَزِمَ
láama	لَامَ	wáladan	وَلَدًا

2. -l- connected to the preceding and following letters

sulúukun	سُلُوكٌ	sílkun	سِلْكٌ
sálisa	سَلِسَ	ráasalaa	رَاسَلَا
siláaħun	سِلَاحٌ	sálaka	سَلَكَ

3. -l connected to the preceding letter only

ráasala	رَاسَلَ	sál	سَلْ
rúsulin	رُسُلٍ	sálla	سَلَّ

4. l standing alone

rasúulun	رَسُولٌ	dálla	دَلَّ
dúwalin	دُوَلٍ	záala	زَالَ

5. láam immediately preceded by káaf has a special form

šáklun	شَكْلٌ	kúllu	كُلُّ
šáakilun	شَاكِلٌ	kaláamun	كَلَامٌ
kálada	كَلَدَ	šákkalaa	شَكَّلَ

Additional examples.

لِزَامٌ دَالٌّ كِلَابٌ

كَلَّلَ تَلَازِمٌ لَكِ

شَكَرَ شَكَا شَكَرَهُ

15. The letter م míim is characteristically a small circle, often merely a dot or a downward break in the line.

1. m- connected to the following letter only

márkazun	مَرْكَزٌ	máwridun	مَوْرِدٌ

makáanun	مَكَانٌ	máaḍin	مَاضٍ
mašrúuʕun	مَشْرُوعٌ	maráakizu	مَرَاكِزُ
márrat	مَرَّتْ	máa	مَا

2. -m- connected to the preceding and following letters

šimáalan	شِمَالاً	lámmaa	لَمَّا
kamáa	كَمَا	mamáaliku	مَمَالِكُ
šámsun	شَمْسٌ	sámman	سَمّاً

3. -m connected to the preceding letter only

lám	لَمْ	súmmun	سُمٌّ
máwsimun	مَوْسِمٌ	sállama	سَلَّمَ
rásmin	رَسْمٍ	lákum	لَكُمْ

4. m standing alone

marsuumun	مَرْسُومٌ	saláamun	سَلَامٌ
láama	لَامَ	kiráamun	كِرَامٌ

Additional examples.

مُرَاسِلٍ	مَذْكُورٌ	مَشَاكِلِ
سَامٌّ	مَوَادٌّ	شَامِلٌ
مَالِ	لِمَاذَا	رَمَى

16. The letter ب báa? is characteristically an upward tooth-like stroke with one dot below it.

1. b- connected to the following letter only

báššarat	بَشَّرَتْ	bíkum	بِكُمْ
baláağun	بَلاغٌ	barlamáani	بَرْلَمانِ
bádwun	بَدْوٌ	biláadun	بِلادٌ

2. -b- connected to the preceding and following letters

lábisa	لَبِسَ	kúbraa	كُبْرَى
kibáarun	كِبارٌ	súbulin	سُبُلٍ
sábban	سَبًّا	mubáaširun	مُباشِرٌ

3. -b connected to the preceding letter only

márkabun	مَرْكَبٌ	sábabin	سَبَبٍ
sálbin	سَلْبٍ	rákiba	رَكِبَ

4. b standing alone

báabun	بابٌ	dárbun	دَرْبٌ
šáriba	شَرِبَ	káððaba	كَذَّبَ

Additional examples.

سَبَّبَ	مَبْرُوكٌ	بَاتَ
بَاشَا	بَرَكَ	سِبَاقٌ
بَرِحَ	كَبَّرَ	بُرُوكٌ

17. The letter ي yáaʔ is characteristically a tooth-like stroke with two dots below it. In handwriting the two dots are usually connected, forming a short horizontal stroke.

1. y- connected to the following letter only

šadíidun	شَدِيدٌ	yáwmun	يَوْمٌ
yakúunu	يَكُونُ	yadúuru	يَدُورُ
yusallimúuna	يُسَلِّمُونَ	baríidun	بَرِيدٌ
yasúuduhu	يَسُودُهُ	yazíidu	يَزِيدُ

2. -y- connected to the preceding and following letters

sáyyidun	سَيِّدٌ	yawmíyyan	يَوْمِيًّا
miiláadun	مِيلَادٌ	láysa	لَيْسَ
maydáanun	مَيْدَانٌ	kabíirun	كَبِيرٌ

3. -y connected to the preceding letter only

káy	كَيْ	rasmíyyun	رَسْمِيٌّ
malakíyyun	مَلَكِيٌّ	yármii	يَرْمِي
maalíyyin	مَالِيٍّ	siyaasíyyun	سِيَاسِيٌّ

4. y standing alone

markazíyyin	مَرْكَزِيٍّ	baladíyyun	بَلَدِيٌّ
wuddíyyun	وُدِّيٌّ	yádrii	يَدْرِي
bašaríyyun	بَشَرِيٌّ	barríyyun	بَرِّيٌّ

Additional examples.

مِيزَانٌ	كَرِيمٌ	وَزِيرٌ
وَكِيلٍ	شِمَالِيّ	لِي
يُشْرِفُ	يَمْدَحُ	يُكَلِّمُ

18. The letter ن núun is characteristically a tooth-like stroke with one dot above it.

1. n- connected to the following letter only

náadin	نَادٍ	nášarat	نَشَرَتْ
názala	نَزَلَ	nuwwáabun	نُوَّابٌ
nawáaḥin	نَوَاحٍ	náala	نَالَ
našáaṭun	نَشَاطٌ	názaʕa	نَزَعَ

2. -n- connected to the preceding and following letters

yanzilúuna	يَنْزِلُونَ	yánšuru	يَنْشُرُ
mánzilin	مَنْزِلٍ	banáahu	بَنَاهُ
munáasibun	مُنَاسِبٌ	mandúubun	مَنْدُوبٌ

3. -n connected to the preceding letter only

yúmkinu	يُمْكِنُ	mín	مِنْ
sákana	سَكَنَ	báyna	بَيْنَ
lán	لَنْ	mákkana	مَكَّنَ

4. n standing alone

múduni	مُدُنِ	yakúunu	يَكُونُ
bayáanun	بَيَانٌ	makáanun	مَكَانٌ
miizáanin	مِيزَانٍ	sinúuna	سِنُونَ

5. The sequence written as nb is often pronounced as mb, as follows:

mínbarun	or	mímbarun	مِنْبَرٌ
yánbusu	or	yámbusu	يَنْبُسُ
ðánbun	or	ðámbun	ذَنْبٌ

Additional examples.

مَنْ	بَيَّنَ	نَوْعٍ
مُمْكِنٌ	نِيرَانٌ	نَاطَ
يُبَيِّنُ	مَنَاصٌ	مِنْبَرٌ

19. The letter ت táa? is characteristically a tooth-like stroke with two dots above it. In handwriting the two dots are usually connected, forming a short horizontal stroke.

1. t- connected to the following letter only

tadbíirun	تَدْبِيرٌ	taláwnaa	تَلَوْنَا
támma	تَمَّ	tamáaman	تَمَاماً
táðkuru	تَذْكُرُ	tílka	تِلْكَ

2. -t- connected to the preceding and following letters

mátaa	مَتَى	tamtáddu	تَمْتَدُّ
taštáriku	تَشْتَرِكُ	dawlatáani	دَوْلَتَانِ
yatímmu	يَتِمُّ	tátruku	تَتْرُكُ
yátluu	يَتْلُو	tutámmimu	تُتَمِّمُ

3. -t connected to the preceding letter only

támmat	تَمَّتْ	náalat	نَالَتْ
káanat	كَانَتْ	dúrisat	دُرِسَتْ
lástu	لَسْتُ	tárakat	تَرَكَتْ
báytun	بَيْتٌ	kúntu	كُنْتُ

4. t standing alone

sayyaaráatun	سَيَّارَاتٌ	ðúkirat	ذُكِرَتْ
márrat	مَرَّتْ	zúrtu	زُرْتُ
záadat	زَادَتْ	sayyidáatun	سَيِّدَاتٌ
kalimáatin	كَلِمَاتٍ	wáddat	وَدَّتْ

Additional examples.

نَزَلَتْ	ذَكَرَتْ	تَدَابِيرُ
دَوْلَتَانِ	تَسْكُنَ	تَلَا
لَيْسَتْ	رَمَيْتُ	زَادَتْ

20. The letter ث θáa? is characteristically a tooth-like stroke with three dots above it. In handwriting the three dots are usually connected, forming a tent-like mark.

1. θ- connected to the following letter only

θáaminun	ثَامِنٌ	θáanin	ثَانٍ
θámanun	ثَمَنٌ	θúmma	ثُمَّ
θábbata	ثَبَّتَ	θuwwáarin	ثُوَّارٍ

2. -θ- connected to the preceding and following letters

miiθáaqun	مِيثَاقٌ	míθlun	مِثْلٌ
tamθíilun	تَمْثِيلٌ	kaθíirun	كَثِيرٌ
yúθbitu	يُثْبِتُ	mumáθθilin	مُمَثِّلٍ

3. -θ connected to the preceding letter only

mákaθa	مَكَثَ	báθθa	بَثَّ
θúlθun	ثُلْثٌ	θáaliθun	ثَالِثٌ

4. θ standing alone

láwwaθa	لَوَّثَ	wáriθa	وَرِثَ
wáariθin	وَارِثٍ	yáriθu	يَرِثُ

Additional examples.

كَثُرَتْ   ثِيَابٌ   مَوْثُوقٌ

وُثُوقٍ   ثَبَتَتْ   ثَلَاثُونَ

21. The letter ه háaʔ does not have any one characteristic form.

1. h- connected to the following letter only

biláaduhaa	بِلَادُهَا	híya	هِيَ
háammin	هَامٍّ	húnaa	هُنَا
ðahábtu	ذَهَبْتُ	hunáaka	هُنَاكَ

2. -h- connected to the preceding and following letters

láhaa	لَهَا	šáhrun	شَهْرٌ
yuhímmu	يُهِمُّ	tamhiidíyyun	تَمْهِيدِيٌّ
mašhúuran	مَشْهُورًا	tahtámmu	تَهْتَمُّ
láhum	لَهُمْ	bíhaa	بِهَا

3. -h connected to the preceding letter only

našaráthu	نَشَرَتْهُ	láhu	لَهُ
sallamáthu	سَلَّمَتْهُ	málikuhu	مَلِكُهُ
mínhu	مِنْهُ	yášbahu	يَشْبَهُ

4. h standing alone

banáahu	بَنَاهُ	murúurihi	مُرُورِهِ
yasúuduhu	يَسُودُهُ	yákrahu	يَكْرَهُ

Additional examples.

مِيَاهٌ	يَهْتَمُّ	هَدَمَتْ
مُهِمٌّ	شَبَهٌ	نَشْكُرُهُ
شَهِيرٍ	هِنْدٌ	هَلْ

22. táa? marbúuṭah

siyáasatan	سِيَاسَةً	dáwlatun	دَوْلَةٌ
šárikatun	شَرِكَةٌ	biziyáaratin	بِزِيَارَةٍ
kálimatin	كَلِمَةٍ	múddatan	مُدَّةً
nášratun	نَشْرَةٌ	sayyáaratun	سَيَّارَةٌ
wizáaratin	وِزَارَةٍ	tamhiidíyyatan	تَمْهِيدِيَّةً

mašhúuratun	مَشْهُورَةٌ	madíinatun	مَدِينَةٌ

All the above words end in the composite letter ة táa? marbúuṭah, which is composed of the letter ه háa? plus the two dots of the letter ت táa?. This composite letter represents the phoneme t. The táa? marbúuṭah occurs only at the end of a word. Note that the sign ً fatḥatáan is placed immediately above the ة táa? marbúuṭah, with no accompanying ?álif (cf. Section 6).

Additional examples.

شُبْهَةٍ	نِيَّةٌ	كَبِيرَةً
مُرِحَمَةٌ	مَادَّةٌ	سَلَامَةٌ

23. hámzah with ?álif

The sign ء hámzah represents the phoneme ?. It is characteristically a small hook-like figure and often appears together with an accompanying ا ?álif, as in the following examples. Note that in such cases the ا ?álif merely serves as a support for the ء hámzah and does not indicate the long vowel aa. The writing of hámzah is taken up in detail in Section 36.

1. hámzah at the beginning of a word

?išráafun	إِشْرَافٌ	?án	أَنْ
?ílaa	إِلَى	?ámsi	أَمْسِ
?umúurun	أُمُورٌ	?áwwali	أَوَّلِ
?ustáaðun	أُسْتَاذٌ	?aðáaʕa	أَذَاعَ
?úmamin	أُمَمٍ	?ínna	إِنَّ
?usbúuʕun	أُسْبُوعٌ	?isláamun	إِسْلَامٌ

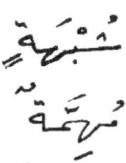

All the above words show the sign ء hámzah with an accompanying ا ʔálif. Note that in these words the phoneme ʔ is (1) at the beginning of a word and (2) is immediately followed by a short vowel. Note that the sign ء hámzah is above the ا ʔálif if the following vowel is a or u, and below it if the following vowel is i.

2. hámzah in the middle of a word

tásʔalu	تَسْأَلُ	ráʔyun	رَأْيٌ
masʔálatun	مَسْأَلَةٌ	šáʔnun	شَأْنٌ
bádaʔat	بَدَأَتْ	ráʔsan	رَأْسًا
saʔáltu	سَأَلْتُ	taʔmíinun	تَأْمِينٌ
taʔákkada	تَأَكَّدَ	taʔkíidun	تَأْكِيدٌ

All the above words show the sign ء hámzah over an ا ʔálif. Note that in these words the phoneme ʔ is (1) in the middle of a word and (2) is either preceded or followed by short a — but not by i or u.

Additional examples.

هَدَأَتْ　　إِبْتَدَأَتْ　　أَلَّذِي

تَأْثِيرًا　　إِذًا　　إِلَّدَ

أَرْسَلَتْهَا　　رَأَى　　إِمْتِيَازًا

24. The letter ف fáaʔ is characteristically a small loop with a single dot above it.

1. f- connected to the following letter only

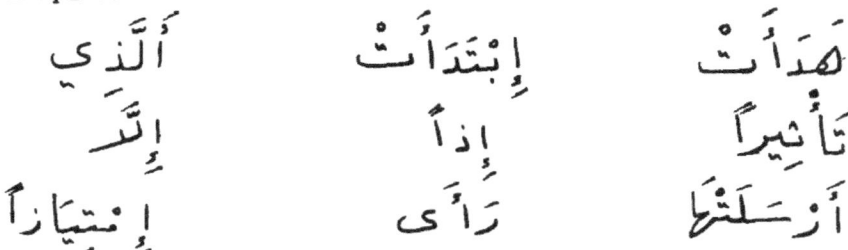

fíihaa	فِيهَا	fáazat	فَازَتْ

wáfdin	وَفْدٍ	fíi	فِي
faarisíyyun	فَارِسِيٌّ	sáafara	سَافَرَ
falláaħun	فَلَّاحٌ	fárraġa	فَرَّغَ

2. -f- connected to the preceding and following letters

káfalat	كَفَلَتْ	yafúuzu	يَفُوزُ
náfsihi	نَفْسِهِ	saffíirun	سَفِيرٌ
ʔalfáaðun	أَلْفَاظٌ	tafáahumin	تَفَاهُمٍ

3. -f connected to the preceding letter only

tataʔállafa	تَتَأَلَّفَ	ʔálifun	أَلِفٌ
sáalifun	سَالِفٌ	kállafa	كَلَّفَ
taʔlíifin	تَأْلِيفٍ	ʔiltáffa	إِلْتَفَّ

4. f standing alone

sáwfa	سَوْفَ	káafin	كَافٍ
ʔášrafa	أَشْرَفَ	ʔišráafun	إِشْرَافٌ

Additional examples.

دِفَاعٌ	أَوْفَدَ	إِلْتَفَتَ
وُفُودٍ	سَفْرَةٌ	فِتْرَةٌ
سُفُنٌ	لَفِيفٌ	فَتِيٌّ

25. The letter ق qáaf is basically a small loop like ف fáaʔ but with two dots above it.

1. q- connected to the following letter only

qád	قَدْ	qáama	قَامَ
qáddama	قَدَّمَ	qaráaran	قَرَاراً
qábla	قَبْلَ	qúwwatun	قُوَّةٌ
fírqatun	فِرْقَةٌ	šárqan	شَرْقاً

2. -q- connected to the preceding and following letters

ʔálqaa	أَلْقَى	taqáddamat	تَقَدَّمَتْ
taqríiruhum	تَقْرِيرُهُمْ	ʔistiqláalun	إِسْتِقْلَالٌ
maqaaláatihi	مَقَالَاتِهِ	ʔalqáwlu	أَلْقَوْلُ

3. -q connected to the preceding letter only

sábaqa	سَبَقَ	wáafaqa	وَافَقَ
ʔaníiqun	أَنِيقٌ	sáabiqun	سَابِقٌ
tafríiqin	تَفْرِيقٍ	ʔittáfaqa	إِتَّفَقَ

4. q standing alone

mawθúuqun	مَوْثُوقٌ	ʔittifáaqun	إِتِّفَاقٌ
yufárriqu	يُفَرِّقُ	sáaqa	سَاقَ
ʔaswáaqun	أَسْوَاقٌ	nifáaqun	نِفَاقٌ

Additional examples

أَلقَرْنُ	دَقِيقَةٌ	يُقالُ
شَرْقِيَّةٌ	مَوْقِفٌ	إِقامَةً
قَدِيمَةٌ	إِسْتِقالَةٌ	وَقْتٍ

26. The letter ج jíim is characteristically a wedge-shaped letter with one dot below it. Note that a preceding letter connects to it from above and to the right.

1. j- connected to the following letter only

jadíidatun	جَدِيدَةٌ	jibáalun	جِبالٌ
járaa	جَرَى	jíddan	جِدّاً
jalsátuhaa	جَلْسَتُها	waʔajáabahu	وَأَجابَهُ
ʔistáʔjara	إِسْتَأْجَرَ	jawwíyyun	جَوِّيٌّ

2. -j- connected to the preceding and following letters

tattájihu	تَتَّجِهُ	natíijatin	نَتِيجَةٍ
fayajlisúuna	فَيَجْلِسُونَ	lájnatun	لَجْنَةٌ
ʔaljálsatu	أَلْجَلْسَةُ	ʔalmájlisu	أَلْمَجْلِسُ

3. -j connected to the preceding letter only

barnáamaju	بَرْنامَجُ	nasíijin	نَسِيجٍ
tatwíijin	تَتْوِيجٍ	yúntiju	يُنْتِجُ

múntajin	مُنْتَجٍ	tadríijun	تَدْرِيجٌ

4. j standing alone

watazáwwaja	وَتَزَوَّجَ	tadárrujun	تَدَرُّجٌ
yanfáriju	يَنْفَرِجُ	mansúujin	مَنْسُوجٍ

Additional examples.

دَرَجَاتٌ	أَلْجَيْشُ	تِجَارِيٌّ
إِنْتَاجٌ	تُجَّارٌ	جَرِيدَةٌ
نَجَاحٌ	أُجْرَةٌ	سَيَجْلِسُ

27. The letter ح ʜáaʔ is exactly like ج jíim but has no dots.

1. ʜ- connected to the following letter only

ʜízbihi	حِزْبِهِ	ʜárbun	حَرْبٌ
ʜáttaa	حَتَّى	ʜadíiθun	حَدِيثٌ
ʜámalat	حَمَلَتْ	ʔiqtiraaʜáatun	إِقْتِرَاحَاتٌ
ʜaflâtuhum	حَفْلَتُهُمْ	ʜukúumatun	حُكُومَةٌ

2. -ʜ- connected to the preceding and following letters

taʜúdduhu	تَحُدُّهُ	ʔalʜárakatu	أَلْحَرَكَةُ
ʔalʜurúubu	أَلْحُرُوبُ	wabáʜaθat	وَبَحَثَتْ
tuʜíbbu	تُحِبُّ	ʔalbáʜru	أَلْبَحْرُ

3. -ʜ connected to the preceding letter only

tásmaʜu	تَسْمَحُ	muráššaʜun	مُرَشَّحٌ
mánaʜa	مَنَحَ	ʔiftátaʜa	إِفْتَتَحَ
tasálluʜin	تَسَلُّحٍ	ráššaʜa	رَشَّحَ

4. ʜ standing alone

ʔiqtáraʜa	إِقْتَرَحَ	maftúuʜun	مَفْتُوحٌ
rúuʜin	رُوحٍ	siláaʜun	سِلَاحٌ
nawáaʜin	نَوَاحٍ	ʔiftitáaʜun	إِفْتِتَاحٌ

Additional examples.

حَيْثُ   مَحَلٌّ   تَوْحِيداً

نَحْوَ   سَمَاحَةٌ   حَوْلَ

إِقْتِرَاحٌ   مُحَادَثَاتٌ   تَحْتَ

28. The letter خ xáaʔ is exactly like ج jíim but with one dot above it.

1. x- connected to the following letter only

ʔalʔaxbáaru	أَلْأَخْبَارُ	xábarun	خَبَرٌ
ʔáxaðat	أَخَذَتْ	xiláafan	خِلَافاً
naaxibúuna	نَاخِبُونَ	ʔaxíiran	أَخِيراً
xaarijíyyatun	خَارِجِيَّةٌ	xárajaa	خَرَجَا

2. -x- connected to the preceding and following letters

bixáyrin	بِخَيْرٍ	sayáxruju	سَيَخْرُجُ
?ittáxaðat	إِتَّخَذَتْ	?intáxaba	إِنْتَخَبَ
muxtálifatun	مُخْتَلِفَةٌ	?alxáaṣṣu	أَلْخَاصُّ

3. -x connected to the preceding letter only

taaríixun	تَارِيخٌ	šáyxun	شَيْخٌ
šámaxa	شَمَخَ	tarsíixin	تَرْسِيخٍ
yársuxu	يَرْسُخُ	máslaxun	مَسْلَخٌ

4. x standing alone

šuyúuxun	شُيُوخٌ	?árraxa	أَرَّخَ
?áxun	أَخٌ	rusúuxin	رُسُوخٍ

Additional examples.

إِخْلَاصٌ	تَأْخِيرًا	أَشْخَاصٌ
يَخْتَلِفُ	إِخْوَانٌ	خَبِيرٌ
رَسَخَتْ	تُخَالِفُ	أُخْرَى

29. máddah

ra?áahu	رَآهُ	?aaθáarun	آثَارٌ

ʔalqurʔáanu	أَلْقُرْآنُ	ʔalʔáana	أَلْآنَ
taʔáamara	تَآمَرَ	ʔáatin	آتٍ
bádaʔaa	بَدَآ	ʔalʔáaxaru	أَلْآخَرُ
ʔáaxaða	آخَذَ	ʔaaláafun	آلَافٌ

All the above words show the sign ‾ máddah over an | ʔálif. This composite letter indicates the sequence ʔ followed by the long vowel aa. This method of indicating the sequence ʔaa is used when the phoneme ʔ is (1) at the beginning of a word or (2) is within a word and preceded by a consonant or by the vowel a.

Additional examples.

مَآدِبُ	آثَرَ	آمَنَ
آخِرٌ	آمَالٌ	مَآكِلُ
آفَاقٌ	آلَمَ	آوِنَةٌ

30. The letter ع ʕáyn is characteristically a small flattened loop.

1. ʕ- connected to the following letter only

dáʕat	دَعَتْ	ʕáadatan	عَادَةً
ʕinda	عِنْدَ	máwʕidan	مَوْعِداً
ʕáqadat	عَقَدَتْ	ʕárabun	عَرَبٌ
ʕálaa	عَلَى	ʔiʕláanun	إِعْلَانٌ

2. -ʕ- connected to the preceding and following letters

ʔalʕarabíyyu	أَلْعَرَبِيُّ	yaʕrifúuna	يَعْرِفُونَ
taʕáawunan	تَعَاوُنًا	šáʕbun	شَعْبٌ
samíʕtum	سَمِعْتُمْ	taʕíišu	تَعِيشُ
báʕda	بَعْدَ	sayaʕúudu	سَيَعُودُ

3. -ʕ connected to the preceding letter only

mánaʕa	مَنَعَ	jamíiʕun	جَمِيعٌ
yuðíiʕu	يُذِيعُ	wáqaʕa	وَقَعَ
tajtámiʕu	تَجْتَمِعُ	máʕa	مَعَ

4. ʕ standing alone

ʔijtimáaʕin	إِجْتِمَاعٍ	ʔaðáaʕa	أَذَاعَ
ðiráaʕun	ذِرَاعٌ	šáariʕun	شَارِعٌ
satuðáaʕu	سَتُذَاعُ	náwʕin	نَوْعٍ

Additional examples.

وَدَعَ	عُمَّالٌ	عَدِيدَةٌ
عَامٌّ	أَعْلَنَتْ	دُعِيَ
تَوْسِيعًا	جَامِعَةٌ	يُعْتَقَدُ
يُعَيِّنُ	مَمْنُوعَةٌ	إِتِّبَاعٌ

31. The letter غ ğáyn is exactly like ع ʕáyn but with one dot above it.

1. ğ- connected to the following letter only

ğádan	غَداً	ğáyruhaa	غَيْرُهَا
ʔağáað̣a	أَغَاظَ	ğáayatan	غَايَةً
ğárban	غَرْباً	ʔağnáamun	أَغْنَامٌ

2. -ğ- connected to the preceding and following letters

lúğatun	لُغَةٌ	ʔalğúrfatu	أَلْغُرْفَةُ
mağlúuṭun	مَغْلُوطٌ	yaštáğilu	يَشْتَغِلُ
yúğliqu	يُغْلِقُ	bálağanii	بَلَغَنِي

3. -ğ connected to the preceding letter only

mabáaliğu	مَبَالِغُ	ʔalmáblağu	أَلْمَبْلَغُ
tafríiğun	تَفْرِيغٌ	tablíiğin	تَبْلِيغٍ

4. ğ standing alone

fáraĝa	فَرَغَ	bulúuğun	بُلُوغٌ
sáağa	سَاغَ	yúfriğu	يُفْرِغُ

Additional examples.

فَرَاغٌ	سَوَّغَ	تَغَيُّرٌ
بَلَغَتْ	مُبَالَغَةٌ	إِنْبَغَى

32. The letter ط ṭáaʔ is characteristically an egg-shaped loop with a vertical stroke above it.

1. ṭ- connected to the following letter only

wáṭanun	وَطَنٌ	ṭaríiquhu	طَرِيقُهُ
ṭabiiʕíyyan	طَبِيعِيًّا	ʔáṭlaqa	أَطْلَقَ
ʔaṭáaqa	أَطَاقَ	ṭayyaaráatun	طَيَّارَاتٌ

2. -ṭ- connected to the preceding and following letters

súlṭatun	سُلْطَةٌ	taṭáwwuran	تَطَوُّرًا
ʔáʕṭaa	أَعْطَى	maṭáarun	مَطَارٌ
yaqṭaʕuhaa	يَقْطَعُهَا	maħáṭṭatun	مَحَطَّةٌ

3. -ṭ connected to the preceding letter only

fáqaṭ	فَقَطْ	náfṭun	نَفْطٌ
ʔalwásaṭu	أَلْوَسَطُ	xáṭṭun	خَطٌّ
muħíiṭun	مُحِيطٌ	ʔalʔáwsaṭu	أَلْأَوْسَطُ

4. ṭ standing alone

lišárṭin	لِشَرْطٍ	ʔinħiṭáaṭun	إِنْحِطَاطٌ
našáaṭin	نَشَاطٍ	xuṭúuṭun	خُطُوطٌ
ʔağláaṭun	أَغْلَاطٌ	ʔaħáaṭa	أَحَاطَ

Additional examples.

يُعْطِي	مَغْلُوطٌ	شُرُوطٍ
أَلْوُسْطَى	يَطْلُبُ	طَاقَةٌ
يَسْتَطِيعُ	خِطَابُهُ	خَطِيرٌ

33. The letter ظ ð̣áaʔ is exactly like ط ṭáaʔ but with one dot above it.

1. ð̣- connected to the following letter only

ð̣urúufun	ظُرُوفٌ	ð̣áhara	ظَهَرَ
manáað̣iru	مَنَاظِرُ	ð̣aahíratun	ظَاهِرَةٌ
ð̣állat	ظَلَّتْ	muwað̣ð̣afúuna	مُوَظَّفُونَ

2. -ð̣- connected to the preceding and following letters

nið̣áamun	نِظَامٌ	ʔintáð̣arat	إِنْتَظَرَتْ
Háafað̣at	حَافَظَتْ	munað̣ð̣ámatun	مُنَظَّمَةٌ
mað̣áahiru	مَظَاهِرُ	ʕað̣íiman	عَظِيماً

3. -ð̣ connected to the preceding letter only

ʔiHtáfað̣a	إِحْتَفَظَ	láaHað̣a	لَاحَظَ
yuHáafið̣u	يُحَافِظُ	ğalíið̣un	غَلِيظٌ

4. ð̣ standing alone

ʜuð̣úuð̣in	حُظُوظٍ	ʔiʜtifáað̣un	إِحْتِفَاظٌ
ʔalfáað̣un	أَلْفَاظٌ	malfúuð̣un	مَلْفُوظٌ

Additional examples.

تَعْظِيمٌ	ظَرِيفٌ	ظَنَنْتُ
مُعْظَمُ	حَظٌّ	إِنْتِظَامٌ
مَظْهَرٌ	ظُهُوراً	أَظْهَرَ

34. The letter ص ṣáad is characteristically a small egg-shaped loop with a small tooth-like mark following the loop.

1. ṣ- connected to the following letter only

ʔalʕaaṣímatu	أَلْعَاصِمَةُ	ṣaadiráatun	صَادِرَاتٌ
ṣárraʜa	صَرَّحَ	ṣaʜíiʜun	صَحِيحٌ
wáṣalat	وَصَلَتْ	laʔáṣbaʜa	لَأَصْبَحَ

2. -ṣ- connected to the preceding and following letters

ʔiqtiṣaadíyyun	إِقْتِصَادِيٌّ	taṣríiʜan	تَصْرِيحاً
maṣáaniʕu	مَصَانِعُ	ʔittáṣala	إِتَّصَلَ
ʔalʕáṣru	أَلْعَصْرُ	máṣdarun	مَصْدَرٌ

3. -ṣ connected to the preceding letter only

xáṣṣaṣa	خَصَّصَ	šáxṣin	شَخْصٍ
ʜíṣaṣun	حِصَصٌ	yağúuṣu	يَغُوصُ

4. ṣ standing alone

ʔašxáaṣun	أَشْخَاصٌ	báraṣun	بَرَصٌ
xuṣúuṣun	خُصُوصٌ	ʜírṣun	حِرْصٌ

Additional examples.

تَحْصِيلٌ حُصُولاً إِخْتِصَاصٌ

يُصَدِّرُ فَصَارَتْ صَلِيبِيٌّ

صُفُوفٌ صُحُفٌ يَصِلُ

35. The letter ض ḍáad is exactly like ص ṣaad but with one dot above it.

1. ḍ- connected to the following letter only

ḍíddun	ضِدٌّ	ḍáğṭun	ضَغْطٌ
mawḍúuʕun	مَوْضُوعٌ	ʔalmáaḍii	أَلْمَاضِي
wúḍiʕa	وُضِعَ	muʕaaráḍatun	مُعَارَضَةٌ

2. -ḍ- connected to the preceding and following letters

ʔáyḍan	أَيْضاً	qaḍíyyatun	قَضِيَّةٌ
ʜáḍarahaa	حَضَرَهَا	ʕúḍwun	عُضْوٌ

máḍaa	مَضَى	Haḍrátukum	حَضْرَتُكُمْ

3. -ḍ connected to the preceding letter only

báʕḍun	بَعْضٌ	ʕaríiḍun	عَرِيضٌ
Háḍḍa	حَضَّ	Haḍíiḍun	حَضِيضٌ

4. ḍ standing alone

ʔaráaḍin	أَرَاضٍ	ʔárḍun	أَرْضٌ
taʕárruḍun	تَعَرُّضٌ	máʕriḍun	مَعْرِضٌ

Additional examples.

قَرْضٌ	تَعَارُضٌ	عَرْضٌ
حُضُورٌ	أُحْتُضِرَ	فَضَّلَ
مَرِيضاً	إِعْتَرَضَ	فَرْضٍ

36. hámzah

This section takes up in detail the discussion of the sign ء hámzah that was begun in Section 23. The sign ء hámzah, which represents the phoneme ʔ, may occur alone or together with one of three other letters. How it is written in any given word depends upon (1) where the phoneme ʔ comes in the word and (2) what vowel or vowels precede and/or follow it.

The letter with which the sign ء hámzah occurs is called the كُرْسِيٌّ kúrsiyy 'seat' of the hámzah. There are three such seats, as follows:

1. An undotted ى yáaʔ
2. A و wáaw
3. An ا ʔálif

A fourth way is hámzah alone without a seat.

These four ways of writing the sign ء hámzah are taken up in the following sections (36.1-5). Note that the letters used as seats have no sound value.

36.1 hámzah with yáaʔ

1. ʔ in the middle of a word

laajiʔúuna	لَاجِئُونَ	súʔimat	سُئِمَتْ
yuhaddiʔúuna	يُهَدِّئُونَ	súʔilat	سُئِلَتْ
natáaʔiju	نَتَائِجُ	bíʔrun	بِئْرٌ
náaʔibun	نَائِبٌ	jíʔtu	جِئْتُ
qáaʔimun	قَائِمٌ	raʔíisun	رَئِيسٌ
súuʔilat	سُوئِلَتْ	riʔáasatan	رِئَاسَةً

All the above words show the sign ء hámzah above an undotted ى yáaʔ. Note that in these words the phoneme ʔ is (1) in the middle of a word and (2) is preceded or followed by the vowel i.

2. ʔ at the end of a word

šawáaṭiʔu	شَوَاطِئُ	hádiʔa	هَدِئَ
láajiʔun	لَاجِئٌ	xáṭiʔa	خَطِئَ
háadiʔin	هَادِئٍ	yúbṭiʔu	يُبْطِئُ

All the above words show the sign ء hámzah above an undotted ى yáaʔ. Note that in these words the phoneme ʔ is (1) the last consonant in the word and (2) is preceded by the short vowel i.

36.2 hámzah with wáaw

1. ʔ in the middle of a word

muʔállifun	مُؤَلِّفٌ	muʔtámarun	مُؤْتَمَرٌ
yuʔáθθiru	يُؤَثِّرُ	masʔúulun	مَسْؤُولٌ
yuʔáddii	يُؤَدِّي	šuʔúunun	شُؤُونٌ
suʔáalun	سُؤَالٌ	báʔusa	بَؤُسَ
tafáaʔulan	تَفَاؤُلاً	yahdaʔúuna	يَهْدَؤُونَ

All the above words show the sign ء hámzah above a و wáaw. Note that in these words the phoneme ʔ is (1) in the middle of a word and (2) is preceded or followed by the vowel u -- but not by the vowel i.

2. ʔ at the end of a word

yájruʔu	يَجْرُؤُ	báṭuʔa	بَطُؤَ
járuʔa	جَرُؤَ	máruʔa	مَرُؤَ

All the above words show the sign ء hámzah above a و wáaw. Note that in these words the phoneme ʔ is (1) the last consonant in the word and (2) is preceded by short u.

36.3 hámzah with ʔálif

1. ʔ at the beginning of a word

ʔújjilat	أُجِّلَتْ	ʔádnaa	أَدْنَى
ʔúxraa	أُخْرَى	ʔajáaba	أَجَابَ

ʔistáwrada	إِسْتَوْرَدَ	ʔúulaa	أُولَى
ʔiiθáarun	إِيثَارٌ	ʔúujida	أُوجِدَ
ʔiijáadun	إِيجَادٌ	ʔintáhaa	إِنْتَهَى

All the above words show the sign ء hámzah with an ا ʔálif. Note that in these words the phoneme ʔ is (1) at the beginning of a word and (2) is followed by both long and short vowels except long aa (for which see Section 29). In such words the sign ء hámzah is above the ا ʔálif if the next vowel is a or u, and below it if the next vowel is i.

2. ʔ in the middle of a word

tásʔalu	تَسْأَلُ	qaráʔtum	قَرَأْتُمْ
masʔálatun	مَسْأَلَةٌ	taʔmíinun	تَأْمِينٌ
taʔállafa	تَأَلَّفَ	yáʔxuðu	يَأْخُذُ
bádaʔat	بَدَأَتْ	šáʔnun	شَأْنٌ
lájaʔat	لَجَأَتْ	máʔwan	مَأْوًى

All the above words show the sign ء hámzah over an ا ʔálif. Note that in these words the phoneme ʔ is (1) in the middle of a word and (2) is preceded or followed by short a (for long aa see Section 29) — but not by the vowels i or u.

3. ʔ at the end of a word

ʔábṭaʔa	أَبْطَأَ	bádaʔa	بَدَأَ
lájaʔa	لَجَأَ	nábdaʔu	نَبْدَأُ
málaʔa	مَلَأَ	ʔibtádaʔa	إِبْتَدَأَ

yáhdaʔu	يَهْدَأُ	yúqraʔu	يُقْرَأُ

All the above words show the sign ء hámzah above an ا ʔálif. Note that in these words the phoneme ʔ is (1) the last consonant in the word and (2) is preceded by short a.

36.4 hámzah standing alone

1. ʔ in the middle of a word

tašáaʔama	تَشَاءَمَ	sáaʔala	سَاءَلَ
ʔisáaʔatun	إِسَاءَةٌ	láaʔama	لَاءَمَ
jáaʔat	جَاءَتْ	tasáaʔala	تَسَاءَلَ

All the above words show the sign ء hámzah standing alone. Note that in these words the phoneme ʔ is (1) in the middle of a word and (2) is preceded by long aa and followed by short a.

2. ʔ at the end of a word

baṭíiʔun	بَطِيءٌ	wuzaráaʔu	وُزَرَاءُ
bádʔun	بَدْءٌ	masáaʔan	مَسَاءً
šáyʔun	شَيْءٌ	jáaʔa	جَاءَ
hudúuʔun	هُدُوءٌ	ʔijráaʔin	إِجْرَاءٍ

All the above words show the sign ء hámzah standing alone. Note that in these words the phoneme ʔ is (1) the last consonant in the word and (2) is preceded by a long vowel or by a consonant. The sign ً fatḥatáan is usually written above such a ء hámzah, as in the second example in the right-hand column, but may also be accompanied by an ا ʔálif as described in Section 6.

36.5 Variant writings of hámzah

šáy?an	شَــيْئاً	or	شَيْئاً
háy?atun	هَيْأَةٌ	or	هَيْئَةٌ
rú?iya	رُؤِيَ	or	رُئِيَ
mí?atun	مِأَةٌ	or	مِئَةٌ
?ijraa?íyyun	إِجْرَاءِيٌّ	or	إِجْرَائِيٌّ
tafáa?ulun	تَفَاءُلٌ	or	تَفَاؤُلٌ

The above words show certain variants in the writing of the sign ء hámzah. The representation of the phoneme ? is complicated by historical considerations and not all dictionaries and texts show complete consistency. The variants usually occur when the phoneme ? is the last consonant in the word or comes before certain endings. In your reading you may expect to find variations that do not precisely agree with the system as set forth here.

Additional examples of the writing of the sign ء hámzah.

إِيصَالٌ	تَأْمُرُ	دَائِرَةٌ
يَقْرَؤُونَ	وِئَامٌ	مُرِئَ
دَقَائِقُ	جَرَائِدُ	هَدَأَتْ
مَسْؤُولَةٌ	هُزُوءًا	إِسْتَأْنَفَ
أَعْضَاءُ	أَصْدِقَاءُ	رَأْسٌ
إِلْغَاءُ	أَنْبَاءُ	إِلْقَاءُ
قُرَّاءُ	دَوَائِرُ	مَبْدَأٌ
زُعَمَاءُ	أَنْبَأَتْ	أَسْئِلَةٌ

37. A special way of indicating long aa

liðáalika	لِذٰلِكَ	háaðaa	هٰذَا
kaðáalika	كَذٰلِكَ	háaðihi	هٰذِهِ
laakínna	لٰكِنَّ	haaʔuláaʔi	هٰؤُلَاءِ
ʔaḷḷáahu	أَللّٰهُ	háakaðaa	هٰكَذَا
lilláahi	لِلّٰهِ	ðáalika	ذٰلِكَ

All the above words show an ا ʔálif, indicating the long vowel aa, placed above a consonant, instead of following it (cf. Section 4.). There are only a few words written in this way; these are the most common.

Note that there is no special letter in the Arabic alphabet to indicate the phoneme ḷ (the next to the last example in the left-hand column).

38. Pause forms

If you have been working through this material with an educated native speaker of Arabic, you have probably noticed that he does not always pronounce the same word in the same way. Such modifications in pronunciation typically involve the omission of final short vowels and nunation (cf. Section 6.). We call a form of a word modified in this way a PAUSE FORM.

A pause form is characteristically shorter than the FULL FORM of the same word. Pause forms occur typically at the end of a sentence, and in the pronunciation of single words in isolation, especially if such words commonly stand at the end of sentences. Within sentences pause forms may occur at the end of a phrase. Where pause forms are used within a sentence, and how often they occur, varies with different speakers and apparently depends upon the style of reading. This means that the same speaker will often read the same passage differently on different occasions.

The following examples will illustrate the modifications that occur to produce pause forms. Note especially that Arabic words are always written in their full form; the pause forms must be supplied by the reader.

1. Words ending in táaʔ marbúuṭah

PAUSE FORM	FULL FORM	
jadíidah	jadíidatun	جَدِيدَةٌ
jadíidah	jadíidatin	جَدِيدَةٍ
jadíidah	jadíidatan	جَدِيدَةً
ʔaljadíidah	ʔaljadíidatu	أَلْجَدِيدَةُ
ʔaljadíidah	ʔaljadíidati	أَلْجَدِيدَةِ
ʔaljadíidah	ʔaljadíidata	أَلْجَدِيدَةَ
qáadimah	qaadímatun	قَادِمَةٌ
qáadimah	qaadímatin	قَادِمَةٍ
qáadimah	qaadímatan	قَادِمَةً
ʔalqáadimah	ʔalqaadímatu	أَلْقَادِمَةُ
ʔalqáadimah	ʔalqaadímati	أَلْقَادِمَةِ
ʔalqáadimah	ʔalqaadímata	أَلْقَادِمَةَ

In pause, words ending in táaʔ marbúuṭah drop final vowels and nunation (cf. Section 6.) and the t is replaced by h. This results in all the pause forms being alike. Note the change in the position of primary stress in the pause forms of the last six examples as compared to the full forms.

2. Words (except those with táaʔ marbúuṭah) ending in a short vowel or nunation

PAUSE FORM	FULL FORM	
jadíid	jadíidun	جَدِيدٌ
jadíid	jadíidin	جَدِيدٍ
jadíidaa *or* jadíidan	jadíidan	جَدِيدًا
ʔaljadíid	ʔ-ljadíidu	أَلْجَدِيدُ
ʔaljadíid	ʔaljadíidi	أَلْجَدِيدِ
ʔaljadíid	ʔaljadíida	أَلْجَدِيدَ
mính	mínhu	مِنْهُ
bíh	bíhi	بِهِ
fíih	fíihi	فِيهِ
biláaduh	biláaduhu	بِلَادُهُ
jíddaa *or* jíddan	jíddan	جِدًّا
kaθíiraa *or* kaθíiran	kaθíiran	كَثِيرًا

In pause, all final short vowels and the endings -un and -in are dropped. The ending -an is either replaced by -aa or remains unchanged. The replacement by -aa is the Classical form; the unchanged form is more common in modern reading.

3. Words ending in a long vowel or a consonant

PAUSE FORM	FULL FORM	
biláaduhaa	biláaduhaa	بِلَادُهَا
ʔalkúbraa	ʔalkúbraa	أَلْكُبْرَى
ʔalmáaḍii	ʔalmáaḍii	أَلْمَاضِي
yátluu	yátluu	يَتْلُو
biláaduhum	biláaduhum	بِلَادُهُمْ
bíkum	bíkum	بِكُمْ
fáqaṭ	fáqaṭ	فَقَطْ
járat	járat	جَرَتْ

In pause, words ending in a long vowel or a consonant remain unchanged.

39. Grammatical considerations

Up to this point we have described the Arabic writing system with a minimum of reference to the grammar of Classical Arabic. That is, we have regarded the problem as one involving the interpretation of the writing system without a knowledge of the grammatical status of the words and forms involved. However, it is necessary to know some grammatical facts in order to interpret certain peculiarities of spelling, and certain modifications of words when they come together within sentences. Most of the following sections will involve such facts.

40. Verb forms with a final ʔálif

tárakuu	تَرَكُوا	ʔajáabuu	أَجَابُوا

kásaw	كَسَوْا	lájaʔuu	لَجَؤُوا
bánaw	بَنَوْا	ʔarsaluu	أَرْسَلُوا
rámaw	رَمَوْا	xárajuu	خَرَجُوا

The above verbs show the endings -uu and -aw meaning 'plural'. After such endings on verbs the writing system shows an ا ʔálif. This ا ʔálif has no sound value. Additional examples:

يَلْزَمُوا	بَلَغُوا	يُسَلِّمُوا
يَتَّفِقُوا	تَلَوْا	إِتَّخَذُوا
يَحْضُرُوا	يَتْلُوا	تَرَبَّوْا

41. The prefix for "the"

Read the first word in the right-hand column and then the corresponding word in the left-hand column. Continue this way down the list.

ʔalkútlatu	أَلْكُتْلَةُ	kútlatun	كُتْلَةٌ
ʔalqáwlu	أَلْقَوْلُ	qáwlun	قَوْلٌ
ʔalʔámru	أَلْأَمْرُ	ʔámrun	أَمْرٌ
ʔalbayáanu	أَلْبَيَانُ	bayáanun	بَيَانٌ
ʔalfúrṣatu	أَلْفُرْصَةُ	fúrṣatun	فُرْصَةٌ
ʔalxábaru	أَلْخَبَرُ	xábarun	خَبَرٌ
ʔalħárbu	أَلْحَرْبُ	ħárbun	حَرْبٌ

ʔalhujúumu	أَلْهُجُومُ	hujúumun	هُجُومٌ
ʔalğáayatu	أَلْغَايَةُ	ğáayatun	غَايَةٌ
ʔalʕádadu	أَلْعَدَدُ	ʕádadun	عَدَدٌ
ʔaljaríidatu	أَلْجَرِيدَةُ	jaríidatun	جَرِيدَةٌ
ʔalmájlisu	أَلْمَجْلِسُ	májlisun	مَجْلِسٌ
ʔalwizáaratu	أَلْوِزَارَةُ	wizáaratun	وِزَارَةٌ
ʔalyáwmu	أَلْيَوْمُ	yáwmun	يَوْمٌ

All the words in the left-hand column show the prefix for "the". In Classical Arabic this prefix has different forms, depending on the first consonant of the word to which it is attached. When the first consonant is one of the following: k q ʔ b f x ħ h ğ ʕ j m w y , the prefix is l- as in the above examples.

When a word having this prefix occurs in isolation or at the beginning of a sentence, the prefix has the form ʔal-. This prefix written as a part of the word to which it is attached and does not affect the position of primary stress.

Note the combination لأ láam ʔálif when the prefix is attached to a word beginning with the phoneme ʔ. The ا ʔálif here does not indicate the long vowel aa.

Additional examples.

أَلْكَافَّةُ	أَلْبَحْثُ	أَلْأَرَاضِي
أَلْوَفْدُ	أَلْحَادِثُ	أَلْجَلَالَةُ
أَلْكَثْرَةُ	أَلْفِعْلُ	أَلْعِبَارَةُ
أَلْهُدُوءُ	أَلْغَرَضُ	أَلْخِطَابُ
أَلْيَمَنُ	أَلْمِنْطَقَةُ	أَلْقَصْرُ

42. Variant forms of the prefix for "the"

ʔattiláawatu	أَلتِّلَاوَةُ	tiláawatun	تِلَاوَةٌ
ʔaṭṭaríiqu	أَلطَّرِيقُ	ṭaríiqun	طَرِيقٌ
ʔaddársu	أَلدَّرْسُ	dársun	دَرْسٌ
ʔaḍḍuyúufu	أَلضُّيُوفُ	ḍuyúufun	ضُيُوفٌ
ʔaθθáanii	أَلثَّانِي	θáanin	ثَانٍ
ʔaððáhabu	أَلذَّهَبُ	ðáhabun	ذَهَبٌ
ʔað̣ð̣úhru	أَلظُّهْرُ	ð̣úhrun	ظُهْرٌ
ʔassáabiqu	أَلسَّابِقُ	sáabiqun	سَابِقٌ
ʔaṣṣufúufu	أَلصُّفُوفُ	ṣufúufun	صُفُوفٌ
ʔaššaháadatu	أَلشَّهَادَةُ	šaháadatun	شَهَادَةٌ
ʔazzáytu	أَلزَّيْتُ	záytun	زَيْتٌ
ʔannáadii	أَلنَّادِي	náadin	نَادٍ
ʔarraʔíisu	أَلرَّئِيسُ	raʔíisun	رَئِيسٌ
ʔallúğatu	أَللُّغَةُ	lúğatun	لُغَةٌ

All the words in the left-hand column show a variant form of the prefix for "the". When the first consonant of the word is one of the following: t ṭ d ḍ θ ð ð̣ s ṣ š z n r l , the prefix is t- ṭ- d- ḍ- θ- ð- ð̣- s- ṣ- š- z- n- r- l- respectively, as in the above examples. That is, the first consonant of the word is doubled.

The Arabic writing system consistently shows the letter ل **láam** in the prefix for "the", and indicates the variants by showing no ° sukúun on the ل láam and by placing a ّ sáddah over the first consonant of the underlying word.

When a word having a variant of the prefix for "the" occurs in isolation or at the beginning of a sentence, the prefix has the form ʔat- ʔaṭ- ʔad- ʔaḍ- etc.

Additional examples.

أَلتَّشْرِيحُ　　أَلثَّمَنُ　　أَلرَّغْبَةُ

أَلدَّعْوَةُ　　أَلشَّعْبُ　　أَلسَّعَادَةُ

أَلزِّيَارَةُ　　أَلذَّخِيرَةُ　　أَلصُّحُفُ

أَلطَّلَبَةُ　　أَلضَّابِطُ　　أَلنِّهَايَةُ

أَللِّوَاءُ　　أَلسَّآمَةُ　　أَلظُّرُوفُ

43. hámzatu‿lwáṣl

All Arabic words that are pronounced in isolation or at the beginning of a sentence with an initial ʔ and a following short vowel fall into one of two classes:

1. Those words that retain the initial ʔ and the following vowel under all conditions.
2. Those words that drop the initial ʔ and the following vowel under certain conditions.

That is, many words that in isolation or at the beginning of a sentence begin with one of the following sequences: ʔi- ʔu- ʔa- appear under certain conditions within sentences without this sequence.

The ʔ that is always retained is called in Arabic hámzatu‿lqáṭʕ. The ʔ that is dropped under certain conditions is called hámzatu‿lwáṣl. Words showing hámzatu‿lwáṣl are discussed below.

43.1 hámzatu‿lwáṣl preceded by words ending in a short vowel

Group I

ʔalqáwlu　　أَلْقَوْلُ　　ʔannahráani　　أَلنَّهْرَانِ

ʔalʕáadatu	أَلْعَادَةُ	ʔalʕárabu	أَلْعَرَبُ
ʔalʔağáanii	أَلْأَغَانِي	ʔistiqaalátuhu	إِسْتِقَالَتُهُ
ʔalḥárbu	أَلْحَرْبُ	ʔarruʔasáaʔu	أَلرُّؤَسَاءُ

Group II

máa báyna‿nnahráyni	مَا بَيْنَ ٱلنَّهْرَيْنِ
wayúmkinu‿lqáwlu	وَيُمْكِنُ ٱلْقَوْلُ
fíi jazíirati‿lʕárabi	فِي جَزِيرَةِ ٱلْعَرَبِ
qáddama‿stiqaalátahu	قَدَّمَ ٱسْتِقَالَتَهُ
máʕa‿rruʔasáaʔi	مَعَ ٱلرُّؤَسَاءِ
fáwqa‿lʕáadati	فَوْقَ ٱلْعَادَةِ
samíʕtum báʕḍa‿lʔağáanii	سَمِعْتُمْ بَعْضَ ٱلْأَغَانِي
qábla lḥárbi	قَبْلَ ٱلْحَرْبِ

All the words in Group I begin with hámzatu‿lwáṣl. The Arabic writing system usually indicates the initial ʔ in such words by the sign ء hámzah. Some texts omit the sign ء hámzah and indicate only the vowel.

Group II shows these same words in phrases preceded by words that end in a short vowel. Here the phoneme ʔ and the following vowel drop, and the omitted vowel is replaced by the final vowel of the preceding word. Such words are joined closely together in pronunciation; we indicate this in our transcription by a curved line (‿) connecting the words involved. The Arabic writing system indicates this by the sign ٱ wáṣlah over the ا ʔálif.

Part of the study of Classical Arabic grammar is learning what words and forms begin with hámzatu‿lwáṣl. The prefix for "the" is one of the most common.

Additional examples.

نَشْرَةُ ٱلْأَخْبَارِ	عِنْدَ ٱلنِّهَايَةِ
أَلْبَحْرُ ٱلْأَحْمَرُ	خِطَابُ ٱلرَّئِيسِ
عَاصِمَةُ ٱلْمَمْلَكَةِ	جَزِيلُ ٱلشُّكْرِ
سَافَرَ ٱلْوَفْدُ	حَضَرَ ٱلْجَلْسَةَ

43.2 hámzatu‿lwáṣl preceded by the prefix for "the"

ʔalistiqláalu	أَلِٱسْتِقْلَالُ	ʔistiqláalun	إِسْتِقْلَالٌ
ʔaliqtiṣáadu	أَلِٱقْتِصَادُ	ʔiqtiṣáadun	إِقْتِصَادٌ
ʔalintidáabu	أَلِٱنْتِدَابُ	ʔintidáabun	إِنْتِدَابٌ
ʔalistixláaṣu	أَلِٱسْتِخْلَاصُ	ʔistixláaṣun	إِسْتِخْلَاصٌ
ʔalistijwáabu	أَلِٱسْتِجْوَابُ	ʔistijwáabun	إِسْتِجْوَابٌ

All the words in the right-hand column begin with hámzatu‿lwáṣl. In the left-hand column these same words appear with the prefix for "the". This prefix has here the form li- (in isolation and at the beginning of a sentence ʔali-). However, many Arabs read such words as if they began with hámzatu‿lqáṭʕ. For example, they would read the first item in the left-hand column as ʔalʔistiqláalu instead of ʔalistiqláalu.

43.3 hámzatu‿lwáṣl preceded by words ending in a long vowel

Group I

máttaa	مَتَى	ʕálaa	عَلَى
dárasuu	دَرَسُوا	ʔílaa	إِلَى

jalsátuhaa	جَلْسَتُهَا	háaðaa	هٰذَا
fíi	فِي	máa	مَا

Group II

ʕála_zziráaʕti	عَلَى ٱلزِّرَاعَةِ
ʔíla_lintixaabáati	إِلَى ٱلِٱنْتِخَابَاتِ
Hátta_ssáaʕati	حَتَّى ٱلسَّاعَةِ
dárasu_lqaḍíyyata	دَرَسُوا ٱلْقَضِيَّةَ
háaða_lmawḍúuʕu	هٰذَا ٱلْمَوْضُوعُ
ma_ttaxaðáthu	مَا ٱتَّخَذْتَهُ
jalsátuha_lʔúulaa	جَلْسَتُهَا ٱلْأُولَى
fi_ššárqi_lʔádnaa	فِي ٱلشَّرْقِ ٱلْأَدْنَى
fi_jtimáaʕin	فِي ٱجْتِمَاعٍ

All the words in Group I end in long vowels. Group II shows words that begin with hámzatu_lwáṣl preceded by the words of Group I. In such cases the long vowel is replaced by the corresponding short vowel. Additional examples.

هُنَا ٱلْقَاهِرَةُ	سَمِعْنَا ٱلْخِطَابَ
مَا ٱسْتُورِدَ	فِي ٱلْمَجْلِسِ
إِلَى ٱلْيَوْمِ	تَبْدَأُ ٱلْإِذَاعَةُ
فِي ٱلْمَاضِي	عَلَى ٱلْأَرْضِ

43.4 hámzatu_lwáṣl preceded by certain words ending in -aa and -uu

xaṭṭáa_ssíkkati	خَطَّا ٱلسِّكَّةِ
waħaḍaráa_ljálsata	وَحَضَرَا ٱلْجَلْسَةَ
manduubáa_lħukúumati	مَنْدُوبَا ٱلْحُكُومَةِ
mustamiʕúu_lħadíiθi	مُسْتَمِعُو ٱلْحَدِيثِ
manduubúu_lħukúumati	مَنْدُوبُو ٱلْحُكُومَةِ

The endings -aa 'dual' and -uu 'plural' (with nouns and adjectives) are sometimes pronounced long before a following word beginning with hámzatu_lwáṣl. This occurs chiefly in a very careful reading style; more often these long vowels are replaced by the corresponding short ones, as described in Section 43.3.

43.5 hámzatu_lwáṣl preceded by words ending in consonants

Group I

ʔiláykum	إِلَيْكُمْ	ʕán	عَنْ
húm	هُمْ	qád	قَدْ
mín	مِنْ	báħaθat	بَحَثَتْ
bánaw	بَنَوْا	báda?at	بَدَأَتْ
manduubáyni	مَنْدُوبَيْنِ	samíʕtum	سَمِعْتُمْ

Group II

ʕáni_lmawḍúuʕi	عَنِ ٱلْمَوْضُوعِ

qádi_ntaházna_lfúrṣata	قَدِ ٱنْتَهَزْنَا ٱلْفُرْصَةَ
báħaθati_llájnatu	بَحَثَتِ ٱللَّجْنَةُ
báda?ati_lmaʕrákatu	بَدَأَتِ ٱلْمَعْرَكَةُ
samíʕtumu_lxiṭáaba	سَمِعْتُمُ ٱلْخِطَابَ
?iláykumu_l?axbáaru	إِلَيْكُمُ ٱلْأَخْبَارُ
húmu_llaðíina sáafaruu	هُمُ ٱلَّذِينَ سَافَرُوا
míni_qtiraaħáatin	مِنِ ٱقْتِرَاحَاتٍ
mína_lqur?áani_lkaríimi	مِنَ ٱلْقُرْآنِ ٱلْكَرِيمِ
bánawi_lmadíinata	بَنَوِا ٱلْمَدِينَةَ
mín manduubáyi_lħukúumati	مِنْ مَنْدُوبَيِ ٱلْحُكُومَةِ

All the words in Group I end in a consonant. Group II shows these same words immediately preceding words that begin with hámzatu_lwáṣl. Here these words add a final vowel, in most cases the vowel i. The word mín has two variants: mína before the prefix for "the" and míni elsewhere.

The treatment of the endings -aw 'plural' and -ay 'dual' (the last two examples in Group II) before a following hámzatu_lwáṣl is uncertain. According to some grammarians they add a final -i, thus: -awi, -ayi. This treatment will be followed here. Additional examples.

مِنَ ٱلْجَنُوبِ	حَدَّدَتِ ٱلشَّهْرَ
وَصَلَتِ ٱلْوُفُودُ	عَنِ ٱلْأَخْبَارِ
دُرِسَتِ ٱلِاقْتِرَاحَاتُ	وَعَلَيْكُمُ ٱلسَّلَامُ
دَعَتِ ٱلْحُكُومَةُ	قَدِ ٱنْتَهَيْنَا

43.6 hámzatu‿lwáṣl preceded by words ending in nunation

Group I

ğárban	غَرْباً	ʔiṣláaħun	إِصْلَاحٌ
šimáalan	شِمَالاً	masʔálatun	مَسْأَلَةٌ
ʔaxíiran	أَخِيراً	ʕán masʔálatin	عَنْ مَسْأَلَةٍ

Group II

ʔiṣláaħuni‿jtimaaʕíyyun	إِصْلَاحٌ ٱجْتِمَاعِيٌّ
masʔálatuni‿qtiṣaadíyyatun	مَسْأَلَةٌ ٱقْتِصَادِيَّةٌ
ʕán masʔálatini‿qtiṣaadíyyatin	عَنْ مَسْأَلَةٍ ٱقْتِصَادِيَّةٍ
yaħúdduhaa ğárbani‿lbáħru	يَحُدُّهَا غَرْباً ٱلْبَحْرُ
wašimáalani‿ljibáalu	وَشِمَالاً ٱلْجِبَالُ
waʔaxíirani‿ntáhati‿ddáwratu	وَأَخِيراً ٱنْتَهَتِ ٱلدَّوْرَةُ

All the words in Group I end in nunation, that is, the endings -un -in -an. Group II shows these same words immediately preceding words that begin with hámzatu‿lwáṣl. Here these words add a final -i. Note that this final -i is not indicated in the Arabic writing system.

43.7 Omission of ʔálif with wáṣlah

lilʔusbúuʕi	لِلْأُسْبُوعِ	lilħukúumati	لِلْحُكُومَةِ
littaʔlíifi	لِلتَّأْلِيفِ	lilijtimáaʕi	لِلِٱجْتِمَاعِ

lirraʔíisi لِلرَّئِيسِ lilʕámali لِلْعَمَلِ

When the preposition لِ li- is added to a word that has the prefix for "the", the ا ʔálif and the sign ٱ wáṣlah of the prefix are omitted.

bísmi‿lláahi بِسْمِ ٱللّٰهِ ʔísmun إِسْمٌ

The word اسم ʔísmun begins with hámzatu‿lwáṣl. When the preposition بِ bi- is added to this word in the above solemn introductory formula, the ا ʔálif and the sign ٱ wáṣlah are omitted. This omission occurs only in the above formula; elsewhere the Arabic writing system shows the composite letter ٱ , as in the following examples.

bísmi‿rraʔíisi بِٱسْمِ ٱلرَّئِيسِ

bísmi ʔaʕḍáaʔi‿nnáadii بِٱسْمِ أَعْضَاءِ ٱلنَّادِي

www.ingramcontent.com/pod-product-compliance
Lightning Source LLC
Chambersburg PA
CBHW080637230426
43663CB00016B/2907
* 9 7 8 1 9 5 6 4 7 8 0 7 5 *